# How to Carry Out Media Interviews

*An Expert Guide to Mastering Radio, TV and Online Interviews*

Evadney Campbell MBE,
Co-founder, Shiloh PR

How to Carry Out Media Interviews

First published in 2018 by Shiloh PR Ltd

Copyright ©Evadney Campbell MBE. All rights reserved.

All rights reserved. Apart from any permitted use under UK copyright law no part of this publication may be reproduced or transmitted in any form or by any means, electronic or mechanical, including photocopying, recording, or any information, storage or retrieval system without permission in writing from the publisher or under license from the Copyright Licensing Agency Limited. Further details of such licenses (for reprographic reproduction) may be obtained from the Copyright Licensing Agency Ltd, Saffron House, 6-10 Kirby Street, London EC1N 8TS

ISBN: 978-1-909389-19-9

Evadney Campbell

*Be aware of how being on television, radio and social media really works; you will win every time*

# Dedication

I dedicate this book to my children and grandchildren. Karen and Anthony I hope this will be part of the legacy which I leave for you all. I want you all to know that no matter how old you are; it is never too late to achieve whatever you can dream. Throughout your lives, I have worked and achieved all my milestone at stages in my life when it would generally be considered to be too late. I hope my determination to do all I want, no matter the challenges will be the motivation you need to go all the way to the sky and beyond.

I want nothing more than give everyone a voice and there is no better way to reach millions than through the media. I pray this guidebook will hold your hand through this journey.

Evadney Campbell

# How to Carry Out Media Interviews

*An Expert Guide to Mastering Radio, TV & Online Interviews*

# Contents

| | |
|---|---|
| **Acknowledgements** | **8** |
| **Foreword** | **10** |
| **Introduction** | **14** |
| **About The Author: Evadney Campbell** | **17** |
| SHILOH **PR** | 18 |
| **Chapter 1** | **20** |
| HOW DO YOU REACH THE MEDIA? | 20 |
| HOW DO I SECURE MEDIA INTEREST? | 25 |
| **Chapter 2** | **27** |
| PREPARING FOR A BROADCAST INTERVIEW | 27 |
| VALUE OF MEDIA EXPOSURE | 27 |
| ALWAYS BE READY! | 29 |
| **Chapter 3** | **31** |
| **THE MEDIA** | 31 |
| *The production team* | *31* |
| *The most appropriate medium for your story?* | *32* |
| *Nothing is: "Off the record"!* | *35* |
| **Chapter 4** | **37** |
| TELEVISION: | 37 |
| RADIO: | 40 |
| DRESS COMFORTABLY: | 42 |
| A FEW SIMPLE TIPS: | 44 |
| ON ARRIVAL WHAT TO EXPECT: | 45 |
| **Chapter 5** | **47** |
| **THE FINAL STAGE** | 47 |
| *Television Studio Layout:* | 47 |

| | |
|---|---|
| *Radio Studio Layout:* | *49* |
| *Skype:* | *50* |
| *Telephone:* | *51* |
| *Vocal Inflection – Your Voice:* | *52* |
| *Eye Contact:* | *56* |
| *Repetition:* | *56* |
| *Remember!* | *57* |

## Chapter 6     58

ADDITIONAL TIPS:     58
RULES TO LIVE BY WHEN DEALING WITH REPORTERS 61

## Some Frequently Asked Questions:     63

## Training Opportunities:     68

CREATING AN EFFECTIVE PR CAMPAIGN: MAXIMISE YOUR BRAND POTENTIAL AND MEDIA PRESENCE     69
HANDLING THE MEDIA DURING A CRISIS     71
INTERVIEWING TECHNIQUES     73
EFFECTIVE CUSTOMER RELATIONS     75

## Consultation Packages     78

## Professional Advice/Assistance     82

## Acknowledgements

This is the most challenging section of this guidebook to write, as I have had so many people who have supported, pushed, encouraged and cajoled me throughout the years, especially those who have always pointed out there was a book in me. This may not have been the book you envisaged but I have finally started the process.

In the absence of being able to mention you all, I will take this opportunity to say, a huge thank you to everyone who has contributed to the delivery of this book.

I also like to express my thanks to all those amazing former colleagues who have happily given me many of the tips included in this guidebook from the journalist's view point.

To **Valley Fontaine,** not only gave me tips, she has also written in the Foreword. **Valley**, thank you. We have spent hours discussing this industry and putting the world to rights. Your time has been truly appreciated.

Special mention also goes out **Andrée Massiah, Kealeboga Diseko, (Lebo) Angie Greaves**, and **Colette Machado,** all former colleagues. Without these wonderful ladies giving me their valuable time and expertise I would not have been so confident to have written this book, a comprehensive tool for everyone undertaking an interview, whether with a broadcast media outlet or print publication.

I cannot write any form of acknowledgement without mentioning **Marcia Malcolm.** Marcia has been a tower of strength, encouraging me throughout this process. She edited each of my attempts and given me valuable feedback and suggestions for improvement. Marcia, you will never know how much your effort has been appreciated.

It is not often a mother gets to thank her child for being an advisor but I have to thank mine. **Karen,** though I do not always take your advice with good grace, your keen eye and suggestions for this book are truly appreciated. I am immensely proud of you and thank you for helping me to achieve yet another one of my goals – I am an author!

# Foreword

*"There are more 'journalists' today than ever before. Citizen journalists are setting up on social media and broadcasting to the world. If you are not hoping to make an income or gain a following you can carry on, but if you want to be respected and thought of as a serious media personality whether it be in the world of social media, podcasts, radio, video or TV, then based on my observation, most people need to invest in some training.*

*This is why I am really pleased this book is being published. Many people will tell you they are a professional and will claim to be an expert in their field but have no evidence or lengthy track record to back it up, but this is not the case for Evadney Campbell MBE. Evadney has worked full time as a TV Radio and Online Broadcast Journalist Producer/ Reporter and radio presenter at the BBC for more than 25 years.*

*She can tell you all you need to know. From how to get that interview to how to conduct yourself not just with the presenter but also how to cultivate the supporting staff, yes the people most ambitious people ignore, the people who, unbeknown to you can make or break your opportunity are often the support staff. I have no hesitation writing the foreword for this long awaited guidebook."* **Valley Fontaine**, BBC Broadcast Journalist & Author of *How to Grow Longer Healthier Natural Hair*, whilst wearing weaves, wigs and braids.

*"When it comes to stamina, integrity, professionalism and sheer passion for life Evadney Campbell MBE comes to mind. Her natural gift for engaging and inspiring others is second to none. Knowing her in a professional capacity and as a personal friend, I recognise all these sides to her.*

*If you want an easy intelligent read, a long-term reference tool and guided media training like no other than this toolkit will be the only one you will need to take you through the 'minefield' of preparing for a broadcast media interview.*

*Authenticity definitely shows itself as a real and important factor throughout this guidebook. The term 'just be yourself' or 'just act naturally' is so often used in terms of public presentation of oneself. Easy to say, yet seemingly, at times, so difficult to achieve, but that is what the best media savvy personalities achieve over and over again. Evadney helps you realise this and more in such a decisive way.*

*This book expertly dissects topics into manageable parts. It is all in the preparation! Looking at oneself in the mirror! Knowing your personality – strengths and weaknesses in order to appear as natural as possible and remain on point are definitely key messages. If you can win an audience, you can capture their loyalty. Whether you are in business or a profiled individual, having loyal subjects is what counts especially when negative media surrounds something you do, have done, or are caught in the middle of. Establishing strong ties with your 'audience' can get you through a multitude of situations. This and many more useful* hints and tips will have you knocking on Evadney's door for more. Handling the media can and should be a positive experience. Knowing how best to do it is only a page turn away." **Marcia Malcolm | AICRAM – The Online Business Support Specialist**

"This guide is invaluable to those new to being interviewed in front of a microphone, and those who wish to brush up on their broadcast skills.

Although you may know your subject inside out, you may not be aware of the ways you can get your points across on-air.

I have worked with Evadney Campbell at the BBC and her broadcasting experience is vast and varied.

From a live short TV interview to a pre-recorded in-depth radio broadcast, Evadney will provide you with the key elements you need for successful media interviews." **Andrée Massiah,** Senior Broadcast Journalist, BBC News

"Getting a media interview is one thing - but knowing what to expect when you get into the media studio is another!" Now you can do exactly that! Equip yourself with the insights of the media studio world that **How to Carry Out Media Interviews: an expert guide to mastering TV, Radio and Online Interviews**, will give you to help you ace an interview.

As a broadcast journalist for more than 30 years, Evadney Campbell will help you understand exactly *how to nail your media interview - and get you invited back again and again as a studio guest!*

*This book is a must-read for all those who are seeking media exposure; those who want to know what being in a studio is really like, as well as those studying broadcast journalism! Be unprepared for your media interview and your "amazing opportunity" will quickly become a wasted one! Well-done Evadney! Your talents never cease to amaze me!"* **Colette Machado**, PR & Content Marketing consultant and former BBC News Online journalist

# Introduction

I was inspired to write this book, "*How to Carry Out Media Interviews: an expert guide to mastering TV, Radio and Online Interviews*" after years of working within communities across the country, particularly those described as 'hard to reach' and seeing so few of them either reflected in the media or attempting to get their stories told through the media.

Seeing the same group of people or individuals being constantly under-represented across most mainstream media outlets across the country saddens me, especially knowing the power and influence of the media. Why shouldn't everyone have equal access to this medium? It is far too simplistic to say it is all down to some form of discrimination. Unfortunately, in many cases, it is because these communities rarely attempt to get their voices heard across the media.

For most of my life I have passionately campaigned against inequality and always tried to be a voice for those who were unable to get their voices heard. This, I believe has been one of the core drivers for this guidebook, "*How to Carry Out Media Interviews: an expert guide to mastering TV, Radio and Online Interviews!*"

Before becoming a professional journalist, I did this through my voluntary roles, campaigning, sitting on influential boards and as a spokesperson for various communities. When I became a broadcast journalist, I began to fully appreciate the power of the media and how it can be used as a vehicle to give a voice to the voiceless.

It was during this period that I realized one of the reasons some people were never heard on mainstream media platforms, was due to the reluctance of the individual to put themselves forward and the fear of carrying out interviews particularly with broadcast outlets.

This, I believed has resulted in the media missing out on some really powerful stories and being more reflective of the society in which we live and the many different voices, views and experiences there are.

The media is a powerful tool through which you can reach millions with your message. Sadly, for too many people, gaining access to the media is still extremely challenging. There are many reasons for this, but in my experience, lack of knowledge around how the industry works is one of the biggest reasons. How do you reach the media? How do get anyone to cover your story? These and many more questions are covered in this guidebook.

It is my intention to offer a book that will dispel the myths surrounding interviews with broadcasters, especially television and radio interviews. This guide will not only help you to carry out the interview itself, it aims to give you an insight into what goes on behind the scenes and being able to feel totally prepared from start to finish.

## How to Carry Out Media Interviews

In this guidebook, I will hold your hand from the moment you are considering undertaking an interview, through to completing the interview itself. I will demystify the process, give you an insight into what to expect at the studios, both radio and television and things to consider ahead of the interview.

# About The Author: Evadney Campbell

Evadney on Channel 5 News

Evadney Campbell MBE is a veteran journalist with some 30 years' experience working for the world's largest news organisation, the BBC. During her long career, she has worked in a variety of roles including radio and TV presenting and news reporting.

Listed as one of the Top 100 British Entrepreneurs by Richtopia.com, Evadney was awarded an MBE honour in 1995 by the Queen of England for her dedication to charity work over a number of years.

Evadney is frequently featured in the media, having appeared on national television across the UK, Jamaica and on radio stations in Nigeria and the Caribbean, as well as being featured in dozens of magazines and newspapers.

## How to Carry Out Media Interviews

During her extensive career, Evadney has interviewed hundreds of people ranging from Prime Ministers to pop stars. She is also a qualified trainer and heads up Shiloh PR's media training programmes. Evadney is currently a visiting lecturer at the University of Arts London where she lecturers on BA Hons and MA PR courses.

Given her vast experience in broadcast news, who better to guide you through the minefield of handling broadcast media interviews, than Evadney Campbell MBE?

## Shiloh PR

Shiloh PR is a public relations and media training agency. They offer PR services and media training to corporations and individuals in senior management and SMEs.

Shiloh PR has delivered international training in Nigeria, the Caribbean and the UK. The company also has a strong track record of producing effective public relations campaigns for arts, entertainment and music events in the UK.

Evadney Campbell MBE and Karen Campbell, can boast over 45 years combined experience in the media, working in TV, digital and radio roles for the BBC and other commercial broadcast outlets. The mother and daughter duo founded the company in 2013.

Co-founder Karen Campbell has held a number of different roles within the media; radio production for a number of years for the BBC, as well as senior roles managing digital and social media content for both commercial media organisations as well as the BBC. She is currently responsible for managing social media strategy for the UK's largest cinema group.

# Chapter 1

## How do you reach the media?

Gaining access to the media takes work and determination. Whilst it is not difficult, it is time consuming and one needs to be patient and recognize that this is an ongoing exercise.

There are dozens of national and regional newspapers with combined circulation of millions per month. In addition, there are hundreds of online broadcast outlets including magazines, and this is just in the UK. Couple these with the dozens of television stations we now have access to, gives you an indication of how important the media is as a means of reaching your target and potential clients.

Figures shown are average circulations for January of each year. All figures originate from the Audit Bureau of Circulations (www.abc.org.uk).

| UK Title | 2017 | 2016 |
|---|---|---|
| The Sun | 1,666,715 | 1,787,096 |
| Daily Mail | 1,511,357 | 1,589,471 |
| Metro | 1,476,956 | 1,348,033 |
| Evening Standard | 887,253 | 898,407 |

| | | |
|---|---|---|
| *Daily Mirror* | 724,888 | 809,147 |
| *Daily Telegraph* | 472,258 | 472,033 |
| *The Times* | 451,261 | 404,155 |
| *Daily Star* | 443,452 | 470,369 |
| *Daily Express* | 392,526 | 408,700 |
| *i* | 266,768 | 271,859 |
| *Financial Times* | 188,924 | 198,237 |
| *The Guardian* | 156,756 | 164,163 |
| *Daily Record* | 155,772 | 176,892 |
| *City A.M.* | 90,319 | 97,259 |

**Source:** www.wikipedia.com, http://bit.ly/2eP7lfa

If you are in business or want to establish yourself as an expert in your field, using the media, whether online or offline is a must. You can achieve this through marketing and advertising but the most cost-effective way is still through effective public relations. It is said, that PR is almost 90% more effective than advertising. The adage of how to differentiate between marketing, advertising and public relations is 'Marketing and advertising is you telling people how great you are, whilst PR is someone else saying you are amazing.' Most people will trust an article they read about your company far more than an advertisement they have seen promoting you.

When you are starting up your business or launching a new product, service or building brand awareness, you want to ensure as many people are talking about you as possible, but with pressure on finance it is not always possible to embark on a major marketing campaign. It is therefore vital that you take advantage of public relations and this will mean knowing how to access the media.

It is fair to say, print circulation, though still impressive, is on the decline (**read also**: Roy Greenslade, *Suddenly, National Newspapers Are Heading for that Print Cliff Fall*, The Guardian, May 2016). This can be attributed to the fact that more and more of us source our news from the Internet. If you include online media outlets, you will agree the media is a vital tool in reaching your clients and generating new clients. If you are diligent, you can generate a range of media coverage.

On the other hand, with so many media outlets available, reaching the most suitable media for your needs can be a challenge! However, this challenge is much easier now with the ease of the Internet.

Google or any other search engine such as, Twitter, LinkedIn, Facebook, Instagram are just a few of the plethora of tools at your disposal to locate and connect with journalists, influencers and increasingly bloggers. It takes time and patience to reach the more specialized media outlets for your needs, so, simply focus on finding a few good ones rather than a multitude.

My advice would be to focus your attention on those that are speaking directly to your target demographics. In the case of many SMEs, these will be your local media outlets or trade publications. As a result of the reduction in circulation, hundreds of local media newspapers have been closed. In addition, the number of local journalists working on those remaining has been severely reduced (**read also**: Richard Sambrook, *Stop Press? Last Words on the Future of Newspapers*, The Independent, February 2017). Although on the face of it, this may seem like a negative it is also an opportunity for you.

Having fewer journalists on the ground to source original stories mean newsrooms locally welcome good story ideas and the opportunity to feature local success stories being sent to them. If you can supply them with good copy, you are much more likely to secure coverage.

As this guidebook is entitled: *How to Carry Out Media Interviews: an expert guide to mastering TV, Radio and Online Interviews*, it is important at this juncture to also document some of the main broadcast media outlets available to you that are desperately waiting for your stories.

In the UK, the BBC dominates the media landscape. Arguably it is also the most influential with ten national networks and over 40 local radio stations including BBC World Service, which broadcasts across the world in 33 different languages. Possibly because we all pay for the BBC through our licence fee, it is also one of the most accessible.

In addition to the BBC's dominance, there are hundreds of commercial radio stations operating across the UK that includes dozens of community radio stations. More recently, as print media circulation declines, there has been a growth in broadcast. This has manifested in a number of local TV stations across the country whose aim is to reflect the local areas that they serve. In addition, with the relative ease and cost-effective means of setting up an online broadcast, getting access to the media couldn't be easier.

As you can see, there is not a shortage of media outlets to which you can offer yourself as a contributor both TV and radio, digitally online and to some stations broadcasting across FM. You can also create your own Podcasts or even setup your own online radio station. You can establish yourself as an expert in your field by offering to speak on your subject or even joining in the dozens of interactive call-in shows.

As well as these proactive ways of reaching the media, you can use professional public relations experts to develop an effective PR campaign and strategy for you to gain media attention and exposure. Using public relations, whether through a professional or by yourself is one of the most cost-effective tools you can use to gain attention and reach millions of potential customers.

At the end of this guidebook, I will give you a few more tips you can use to reach these media.

## How do I secure media interest?

As I have stated earlier, the media wants to hear from you. They are open to receiving your stories but you will need to ask yourself some key questions ahead of pitching your story.

Firstly, what is your Unique Selling Point (USP)? This doesn't necessarily mean you are the only one offering this product or service. What you need to identify is what makes your product or service different from the others out there.

Think of your reason for creating the product or even offering your service. Maybe your journey is the story; think about some of the challenges you have had to overcome so far. This is your story and it could be of interest to the media. When you are approaching the media to secure exposure, they are not obliged to promote you but, if you present them with an interesting and engaging story, they will really want to feature it.

Think why would anyone be interested in your story? If you saw a headline for your story, would you want to read it? If your honest answer is no, then think why should anyone else want to hear about it.

If you know your story is worthy, i.e. getting that product or service out there could impact on other people's lives, then think how you can bring it to life. Later in this book, I give you some examples of what you need to consider before deciding which medium is best for you to showcase your story.

## How to Carry Out Media Interviews

If you honestly answer these few questions above, and are able to offer your story to the most appropriate outlets, once you have carried out your research, you are more likely to be successful in getting the media to feature your story.

More tips at the end of this guidebook.

# Chapter 2

## Preparing for a broadcast interview

*An interview with a major radio or television station could either make or break your company!*

## Value of media exposure

I cannot over stress this point. Securing an interview could give you exposure to millions of potential customers. It is a priceless opportunity, but if it is not handled well it could also cost you and your company's future. Poorly handled interviews could destroy your personal credibility, ruin your company's brand and in the worst case scenario, lead to the demise of your business.

## How to Carry Out Media Interviews

The key to ensuring you capitalize on this opportunity is to prepare well, research well and practice, practice, practice ahead of approaching the media or accepting any invitation to appear in the media. If necessary, seek and undergo any formal training you may require from a professional before getting in front of that microphone or camera for the first time.

Your time in the spotlight could be as short as 15 to 30 seconds and highly unlikely to be longer than three minutes in total, particularly if you are being interviewed for television. Forget the old adage – 'Your 15 minutes of fame'. You need to make every second of your three minutes' count. Your aim is to ensure you deliver your message effectively. You want to establish your credibility, raise your profile, build brand awareness and you want to reach your target audience, which in turn, will hopefully help you to convert them into paying customers.

This Guidebook - *How to Carry Out Media Interviews: an expert guide to mastering TV, Radio and Online Interviews,* has been compiled to give you practical tools and tips to help navigate the tricky world of broadcast media. It is a guide for handling interviews in either live or pre-recorded situations for which the audio will be broadcast at a later time or date. Much of the advice also applies to interviews being carried out for print media.

- When we refer to broadcast interviews, we will generally mean an interview that is being conducted for a television, radio programme or video for online broadcasting - something that is becoming much more popular and is set to continue growing. This could be as part of a news item or being part of a panel discussion where you will be included as a contributor because of your knowledge and skills, as an expert in your field, or as a commentator.

## Always be ready!

- In general, if you are being interviewed for a news item on television or radio, it is likely to be with very short notice unless you trigger the interview because you want to promote a product or service. If, however, you are being asked to appear as part of a news item because of your expertise, you will often only have a few hours' notice, especially if you are there as a result of a breaking news story. The limited notification will mean you will have less time in which to carry out any research or preparation ahead of the interview.

- For some people, being called to conduct an interview for television or radio broadcast can be exciting. For others, even when initiated by themselves it can be a very nerve wracking experience.

- The key to dealing with either of these emotions and situations is to be clear about why you are doing the interview, knowing your subject and being clear on what you want to say and achieve. What is your end goal?

- Depending on your perspective, the presence of a camera frequently changes the dynamics between you and the reporter. The camera can be intimidating. Even if in real-life you are a confident person, being placed in front of a camera can affect your confidence.

- There are many factors that you will need to consider before an interview with a broadcast media and these will be covered later.

# Chapter 3

## THE MEDIA

**The production team**

- It is worth noting that broadcast news reporters, whether they are working for a TV station, or for a radio station, typically work to extremely tight deadlines. Some may well be working on several news items at a time. This means the reporter will often have little time to research a subject (particularly when working on breaking news). They will rarely have expertise in your specific field, but will be expected to produce visually captivating and engaging reports that directly impact their viewers.

- Television reporters generally work with a producer. The producer will often do the initial background research and conversation with the interviewee. This means, the individual you initially speak to on the phone may not be the reporter carrying out the news piece. A golden rule here is to never assume you have already given them vital information about you, your company, your product or your area of speciality. Repeat it again if necessary.

- On the other hand, radio reporters will generally be expected to produce and report on the item single-handedly. Also, be aware that if the radio and television company are operated by the same organisation, do not assume the reporters speak to each other. You may even find yourself repeating the same information several times. The golden rule here is to be consistent with your message. What is your end goal?

- In a live situation, for both radio and television, the presenter will carry out the interview. Depending on the size of the media outlet, the presenter may only be operating from briefing material supplied by the researcher/producer. For smaller more local broadcast media outlets, the presenter may be producing the items and you may have already spoken to them ahead of the live broadcast.

## The most appropriate medium for your story?

- On the whole, television news pieces are typically no longer than two or three minutes long. Radio can, and frequently is much longer. On radio, you are able to give a little more of the background story and allow the story to develop during the interview. It is still good practice to keep your answers short and to the point.

- Remember, pictures drive television whereas, the strength of the story being told, or the character of the person being heard drives radio. For television, think, 'picture is king'. To tell your story using television, the picture is far more powerful than the words. This is why it is vital you have strong images to accompany your story. If you are approaching the media for coverage, it is vital you are clear on whether television or radio is the most appropriate medium through which to convey your message.

- Consider whether your story can be told through pictures or if it would be better told through audio. If your story is colourful and can be effectively told with strong images, go for television. If the story is interesting but there are limited pictures to get the best out of your story, think radio. If you are opting for radio, have someone who is knowledgeable, passionate and able to bring your story to life through interview.

Here are a few ideas:

| Idea | Television | Radio | Print |
|---|---|---|---|
| • Product Launch | • Possible (depends on product) if your product has strong images TV maybe the most effective way to give it exposure. | • Possible especially if it has a strong story behind its development. Make sure the person promoting it, is knowledgeable, passionate and engaging. They will need to 'bring the product to life' with just their voice and ability to create a visual image or emotion around your product. | • Highly likely (find an interesting story angle). This could be the developer of the product's story or the story behind the product itself. |
| • Music | • On the day – | • Guests ahead | • Guest |

# How to Carry Out Media Interviews

| Idea | Television | Radio | Print |
|---|---|---|---|
| Concert, Festivals | ahead of the event as long as you have pictures. Past videos etc. or give the TV station access to film at rehearsal ahead of concert/festival. If you have a celebrity as part of your event, they maybe sufficient to generate TV interest in a personal feature etc. | of event/ Obtain reviews | ahead of event. Obtain Concert/ Festival reviews |
| • Book Launch | • Less likely, unless the author has a strong personal story and can then be interviewed as a guest. If the author is unknown, you would need to have a strong image to attract TV attention. | • Yes. Ensure speaker is engaging | • Yes. As for product launch |

# Nothing is: *"Off the record"*!

- For the purpose of this guidebook - *How to Carry Out Media Interviews: an expert guide to mastering TV, Radio and Online Interviews?* We will assume that the interview you are about to give is for positive purposes and not due to a crisis. It could be to promote a new product or service, highlight your leadership or in relation to a current news issue that connects with your business or has been initiated by you as part of your PR campaign.

- If you are carrying out a 'live' interview – this means the interview is being broadcast as you speak; this does not mean this will be the only opportunity for it to be heard. With the current pressures on the media, a single interview is frequently used across several different mediums and in a variety of formats. Remember – what is your end goal?

- In addition, with the influence and importance of the Internet and the speed of social media, broadcasters will want to use your interview to drive traffic to other social media outlets. This is true whether you are being interviewed for a single clip that will be included in a bigger news piece (package), live on air, or pre-recorded for broadcast at a later date. Always think about how it will be used, on Twitter for instance, or picked-up and quoted by other journalists in a blog, newspaper or other news outlet on a related topic.

- If the journalist says they are only looking for a clip (sound bites) for a piece, they may still put your full interview on their website afterwards, so ensure your entire interview is exactly as you would like it to be heard.

- Be warned - Nothing is Off Record. If you accept this, you are unlikely to go wrong. Once a microphone is either clipped on you or placed in front of you, assume you are being recorded. It is easy to forget and say things you do not wish to be made public. The journalist is always listening for anything that makes the story more interesting.

# Chapter 4

## YOU ARE ALMOST THERE

## Television:

*Despite the growing strength of social networks, television advertising is still the most influential medium in people's purchase decisions.* **Source:** www.smallbusiness.chron.com (The Influence of Television Advertising, http://bit.ly/2BPYszA)

- I mentioned earlier the importance of a visually compelling TV piece. As social media becomes more and more prolific with easy access by everyone, we can be forgiven for thinking the influence of traditional media outlets like television and radio have diminished.

- There has never been a greater time for ordinary individuals to access broadcast media as it is today. As long as you have a smartphone you have the ability to reach billions of potential clients using social media. But despite these growing sources of media outlets, the influence of television is still indisputable.

*"Traditional TV consumption accounts for the greatest amount of time spent with media in the UK. In 2016, UK adults will spend an average of 3 hours 8 minutes viewing TV content on a television set, eMarketer predicts. No other single media activity will come close to this figure."* **Source:** www.eMarketer.com (How Traditional Viewing Habits Influence the UK's Digital Video and TV Landscape, http://bit.ly/2EbFA38)

This is as true for the UK as it is in the US. *"A report from the Television Bureau of Advertising and Knowledge Networks Inc. reveals that 37 percent of television viewers make purchase decisions after watching advertisements on television compared to 7 percent for social networks."* **Source:** www.smallbusiness.chron.com (The Influence of Television Advertising, http://bit.ly/2BPYszA)

- If you are being interviewed as a result of a press release about the launch of your new product or service, please make the reporters' life easy. Think ahead about the visuals they can use to illustrate your story. If possible, supply anything you can ahead of the interview.

- At the point of the interview, the reporter will need extra footage (pictures) to help put your story together. You may therefore be asked to film some 'cut-aways' (CU) or GVs (general views). These are images they can use to cover their voice-over when they are narrating your story. Here are some of the most commonly used GVs.

- Sitting and tapping away at a computer or at your desk reading a manual.

- Walking and looking at your new product, picking up pieces, examining them.

- Walking 'through the shot' e.g. walking across the camera until you are no longer in view.

- These will feel really unnatural, so the best way to ensure you feel less conspicuous, practice them beforehand, so you can feel more comfortable and make it appear less staged.

## Radio:

*"More than 90 years after its introduction …. to this day, approximately 92% of consumers aged 12 years or older listen to radio each week."* **Source:** www.justmedia.com (Why Radio Is Still Relevant In A Digital Age, http://bit.ly/2k9Hx6p)

- Contrary to popular belief, radio is still a very influential medium. That is not to say, like the rest of the media world, it has not also suffered in terms of popularity. However, with the introduction of the web, radio has found a new delivery platform.

- Whatever your interest, there is a radio station catering to your needs online. Through the growth of podcasts this broadcast medium is still holding its own. In addition, the radio lives on through our cars; probably the single most prolific listening environment.

- Unlike television, for radio the strength of the story and the person telling it, is what will grab the listeners' attention. It is important to ensure the person telling your story is knowledgeable, believes in your story and is engaging.

- As a rule, though this is getting rare. All the listener has is the voice of the person telling the story. I say getting rare because more and more radio programmes are not only broadcasting across the airwaves, they are being streamed, filmed or recorded to be shared at a later date as a podcast or short video on other online platforms like websites.

- Although the interviewer is being filmed, I still advise that your voice and how you express yourself is the most important thing. How you look or your body language is less important when it comes to being interviewed on radio. It is vital that you pay attention to the strength of your story.

- If your subject is complicated, try to describe it as if you are explaining it to a friend, someone not in your industry – without dumbing it down! Let your charm and personality shine through. You need to be warm, expressive and engaging. Try to be descriptive. Paint a picture with the description of your project. You want the listener to be able to visualise your product or become excited about your service.

- It is recognised that for advertising purposes, radio can be even more effective than television if you can get the listener to create an emotion to your product.

- In both cases, whether you are being interviewed for television or radio, enjoy the experience. Try to smile when being interviewed. Smiling will make you sound much warmer to the listener. More importantly - be yourself!

## Dress comfortably:

- Although this may sound unnecessary, I firmly believe if you are comfortable in how you look and feel you will be able to concentrate on delivering your message without being distracted.

- If you get the opportunity, do a little research on the specific programme you will be appearing on ahead of the interview. Take a look at the style of dress for the presenter and guests. How formal are they? Is it more business like? Will you be sitting or standing? If you are sitting, will it be on a sofa or those 'bar stool' styled seats?

- Think carefully about the clothes you wear. As a woman, when you are sitting down, you do not want to be worried about whether you are showing more than you are comfortable with. As a man, the television studio is extremely hot; you do not want unsightly sweat patches on your shirt. You may be interviewed outside the studio, in this case, the weather may play a part in your choice of clothing.

*What you wear may not be the most important thing when you are appearing on TV, but getting it right will make the experience more enjoyable.*

- The key advice here is to do your research. You can find out by watching past broadcasts of the programme itself, or you can ask pertinent questions when the research/producer calls you to arrange the interview.

## A few simple tips:

- Wear clothes that are neat, clean and comfortable. Even if the outfit looks great on you, if you are uncomfortable it will show in your demeanour or body language. Do not wear anything psychedelic, or too bright.

- Avoid distracting patterns and be careful of some stripes – they do not always work well on camera. I know some people say avoid the colour Green because of the use of 'Green Screen' in a television studio; but I say, it depends on the shade of green you have chosen or whether you are likely to be filmed in front of a green screen.

- Despite my warning above with regard to wearing 'loud' colours, for women, sometimes a bright colour can really enhance your appearance. Try to avoid wearing all black though. I know many of us are worried about the old saying that 'the camera puts 10lbs on you' and feel that the colour black will make you look slimmer; I would still say, you should inject some colour in your wardrobe even if you do have to pair it with something black to make you feel more comfortable.

- Avoid long dangling earrings as these can affect sound quality. The microphones in both radio and television studios are very sensitive and will pick up sounds you may not personally hear or notice yourself.

- Let your personality shine through - your clothes are not being interviewed, you are!

- If you have long or very big hair, I would recommend you wear it pulled back, particularly if you are being interviewed outside - an ill-timed gust of wind can make your hair more of the interview subject than what you are trying to convey.

- Notwithstanding the advice on clothing above, try to match your wardrobe with your role. No one expects the CEO of a construction company to be wearing a navy pinstriped suit, unless of course, that is how you feel comfortable. Your clothes can and should support your message. Be warned though, trying to sneak in a little ad for your company, via a badge or logo, may not be welcomed, especially if you are being interviewed by a commercial media outlet.

## On arrival what to expect:

- This will differ from programme to programme or media outlet; the general arrangement is that when you arrive at the reception you will be collected by the producer of the item or an assistant. If you are being interviewed on television, you will be taken to a waiting room (the green room) where you will be 'walked through'

## How to Carry Out Media Interviews

what to expect, and be given an idea of the questions to be covered. You may even be introduced to the presenter beforehand. In some instances, you may not see anyone else until just before you are about to go on air. Do not panic! Newsrooms are really busy places especially ahead of live broadcasts.

- Try to arrive at least 15 minutes early for radio and much earlier than this for TV. You will need to be prepared for the studio and have your microphone (mic) connected. A little tip here for the ladies, try to wear a dress with a belt, blouse with buttons at the front or a blazer/jacket for easier positioning of the wireless mic.

- For TV you may also need to be prepared by the make-up person. For smaller television stations, there may not be a professional make-up person available. In this instance I would advise putting on your own favourite make-up before arrival. If you are early enough, you can always touch up before going on air. Do not forget a hairbrush.

- Arriving early will also help you stay calm before being taken on-set for the live interview. You do not want to be flustered ahead of a live broadcast. This can result in you losing your train of thought or not being able to deliver your message effectively.

Evadney Campbell

# Chapter 5

## THE FINAL STAGE

**Television Studio Layout:**

- If you have watched any news programme at home, on arrival you will probably be surprised at the actual size of the studio. It is often much smaller than you envisaged. For large news organisations there will be a number of cameras in the studio. Many will be unmanned. They do work, they are just being remotely controlled.

- The general advice here is to ignore the cameras; you are speaking to the presenter so just look at them. Think, you are just having a conversation. Try to forget the cameras are there, unless in very rare situations when you will need to speak directly into the camera. We will discuss this later.

- Television studios have lots of huge lighting. This makes them extremely hot, hence the earlier advice about comfortable clothing. To help, it is advisable you carry tissues or a handkerchief. This will help you if you find yourself sweating on camera. A handkerchief is much better as tissues tend to fray when damp and may leave bits on your skin.

- Once you get into the studio, there will be a 'floor manager' in most TV studios. This will be the person who will advise you where to sit, brief you on how the interview will be carried out and generally assist you with any information needed ahead of going live. In many larger television studios, microphones may be fixed to the desk, so once they have seated you they will simply clip the microphone onto your clothing. If you are wearing a blazer/jacket, this will be great for hiding any loose wires.

- With the growth in interviews being carried out via Skype, for these interviews and as described below, you will need to look directly at the camera at the top of your screen. Try not to let your eyes wander too much.

## Radio Studio Layout:

- Radio studios are in most cases less intimidating than television studios. They will normally only have desks with the presenter and guests sitting in the same space together. On some occasions especially where there are a number of contributors, you may be sitting in a studio separate from the presenter. On the whole, radio studios are much more intimate.

- Not all stations have a production team or someone separately controlling the output. This means the presenter may also be responsible for operating the equipment. Once again, you are just having a conversation, relax, smile, be yourself and enjoy the experience.

## Skype:

- Carrying out television interviews via Skype is becoming more and more popular. Firstly, find a quiet place where you are unlikely to be disturbed or distracted. You do not want to be faced with the unfortunate situation Professor Robert Kelly found himself in when he was carrying out an interview with the BBC and his children invaded the office.

- It is often difficult to look directly into the camera as mentioned when you are being interviewed via Skype but, do try to look directly at the screen and not look around too much.

- Test the equipment before going live. Ensure you have strong Internet connection/signal, headphone and microphone. There is nothing worse than watching an interview, which keeps pixelating, or buffering throughout so make sure you have a strong signal.

- Try to be yourself. **Smile** (not too much – you do not want to scare anyone).

- Try to make **eye contact**. You can do this by looking into the camera.

- Watch your posture. **Sit up straight**.

- As you are being seen, **use non-verbal cues** like nodding. This is particularly useful where there has been a delay between you and the studio.

## Telephone:

- As with television interviews more frequently being carried out via Skype, radio interviews are often conducted via the telephone, in fact they are becoming even more popular than studio based face to face.

- Here are a few tips to ensure you get the most from your interview whether, face to face or on the phone.

- Make sure any nearby radio or TV is turned off. This will help avoid feedback during the interview or any background interruptions.

- Do not use your speakerphone. Whilst you may be able to hear the interviewer, they may struggle to hear you clearly. You want to ensure you get your message across and not be misquoted due to inaudibility.

- Standing up will make you sound much more authoritative and inject energy into your voice, so if possible, it maybe better to conduct your interview whilst standing.

- Make sure you use varying tones in your voice. Let us discuss Voice inflection.

## Vocal Inflection – Your Voice:

*Try to inject some inflection to your speech*

- I mentioned above, the importance of being yourself when being interviewed for radio. This is true for any broadcast interview. Nothing kills a good interview quicker than a monotonous tone of voice. Try to inject some inflection to your speech. A flat tone of voice could make it difficult for the reporter to identify the best clips for later use, or even the key points you are making when they are in the editing room.

- The above is even more important when conducting radio interviews. As highlighted earlier, you must engage and capture the listener - you do not want to lose them because you are boring. Your voice is all they have to go by. Be your charming self. Try not to let your nerves get the better of you.

- Your tone should reinforce the fact you are excited, passionate, concerned and engaged - in other words, you want to back up what you are saying with how you are saying it. You should not conduct the interview in hyper-drive of course, but when you have a point that is important to you, your tone of voice should reflect it. Be mindful though, when you are nervous you may speak a lot faster, slow down a little, especially if you have a strong accent. If you have a soft, quiet tone, practice speaking louder beforehand so it feels more natural.

- It is normal, when you are nervous, that your tone will change. Your own voice won't sound normal or natural to you in playback. Try practicing what you want to say in advance, especially if there are specific words or phrases you want to emphasize.

How to Carry Out Media Interviews

**Hand Movements and Body Language:**

*The way you move during an interview can animate the discussion in a way that supports your point of view and credibility*

- It used to be said that you should not use too many hand gestures in a television interview. This resulted in many people simply looking stilted, uncomfortable and wooden. Whilst I say be careful of waving your arms around too much, you do not want to distract the viewer, it is perfectly acceptable to use hand gestures if it is your normal way of expressing yourself.

- Like vocal inflection, hand gestures and body language are very important. The way you move during an interview can animate the discussion in a way that supports your point of view and credibility. This is as true for a radio interview (surprisingly) as it is for TV; often, if your hands are animated, your voice will follow. For radio, smile when speaking – it really helps. The listener will feel the warmth in your voice.

- Practice can help you here. Practice speaking in front of a mirror to see how animated you are when speaking. If necessary, minimise your hand gestures but see what works for you.

- For TV interviews, you should also practice delivering your message while standing and sitting. A conversation standing up will feel different and you need to be prepared for the intensity. If you are sitting, be careful not to swivel in your chair, rock back and forth, or lean away from the reporter. All three habits are distracting and could undermine the audience's trust and confidence in you.

- If you are being interviewed in a radio studio, avoid tapping your fingers or any implement against the desk – this too is extremely distracting for the listener. Once again, avoid rocking back and forth or swivelling in your chair. If you do this, you could affect the sound quality as you move away from the microphone.

## Eye Contact:

- As mentioned earlier, for TV interviews, whether pre-recorded or live, look at the journalist not at the camera, unless advised otherwise by the reporter. Remember you are just having a conversation with the reporter. If you think of it this way, you will not be worrying about which camera you are being shown on.

- Sometimes, you will be interviewed 'down a line'. This means you may be placed in an unmanned studio in front of a camera – you are on your own or you may just be placed in front of a camera in the corner of a newsroom in another location. On these occasions, the reporter will be in another studio so you will not be able to see them. Look straight into the camera. Try not to look up into the air, down at your feet or look around too much when speaking as this can make you look shifty and untrustworthy to the viewer. If you are asked what you perceive to be a dumb or unexpected question, please, do not roll your eyes!

## Repetition:

When carrying out pre-recorded interviews, particularly for television, you may be asked to repeat an answer. This could be for a number of reasons. Sometimes it is because you are being filmed from different angles. If this is the case, do not change your first answer. Try to be consistent. In the edit, they may want to use bits from both responses to show you from a different angle.

Sometimes being asked to "do that again", may be because your first response was great but a little too long for editing purposes – remember the 15-30 sec rule? In this instance, the interviewer will usually guide you on how you can rephrase your answer. Remember though, it is your message so if you are rephrasing it, ensure you do not lose the essence of what you want to say. Try to refrain from saying, "as I said before"!

## Remember!

No matter how many times you have been interviewed on television or radio the experience can be intimidating. Even though I have carried out numerous interviews for both radio and television, whenever I am being interviewed, I still get nervous. The primary advice I would give is to practice, practice, and practice again and seek professional assistance. The adage, 'practice makes perfect' really is true.

If you plan on appearing on screen frequently, I would also highly recommend that you find a qualified media trainer to conduct mock interviews on camera. Doing this will give you the chance to watch your performance back and identify what worked and what did not. It will also help you to identify any habits you would rather not expose on screen. An outside eye to help you identify verbal and physical ticks that could limit your effectiveness might also be very useful.

If you adhere to all the above, your media interview should be plain sailing. Go enjoy, and capitalize on this amazing exposure.

# Chapter 6

## Additional Tips:

| Do's | Don'ts |
|---|---|
| Have your three key messages clear in your mind.<br><br>• Be able to deliver in 30-40 secs 'soundbites'. | • Don't be late<br><br>• Arrive at least 15 mins early |
| Prepare beforehand:<br><br>• Carry out mock interviews with someone.<br><br>• Fine-tune your message to ensure you can get them across within the time.<br><br>• Prepare for challenging questions too. There may be curveballs thrown at you. | • Don't forget, you are being recorded/broadcast<br><br>• Nothing is completely 'off the record'. Once you have had your microphone placed on you or in front of you – be self-aware. |
| Do your research:<br><br>• Understand the nature of the show you are going on<br><br>• Find out the angle of the story<br><br>• Will you be on your own or | Don't let what you wear or look like be a distraction.<br><br>• Busy clothing, dangling or excessive jewellery can be distracting, leading the audience to focus more on this rather than your |

| Do's | Don'ts |
|---|---|
| part of a panel? If you are on a panel, who are the other panellists?<br><br>• Who is the interviewer, what's his/her style of interview? Will the interview be challenging or entertaining?<br><br>• Find out about the audience i.e. their target.<br><br>A little tip - interviews will generally follow the "what, when, why, where, how" formula. When you do your practice for this scenario, throw in a few 'What ifs?' | message.<br><br>• Narrow stripes are not recommended as they often create a strange effect on camera. |
| Do try to bring some of your own experience into your answers. This helps to personalise it and where appropriate it will demonstrate your expertise in that field. | Don't risk an embarrassing phone moment<br><br>• Turn your phone off or put it on silent; |
| Be clear<br><br>• If you have a complicated specialist area and are being featured on a mainstream show, try to break things down as if explaining to a 10-year-old, | Don't read from your script<br><br>• Unless you are quoting stats or reading an official statement;<br><br>• Don't make more than one point in your |

## How to Carry Out Media Interviews

| Do's | Don'ts |
|---|---|
| without being patronising! <br><br> • Speak slowly and clearly. | answer |
|  | Don't panic <br><br> • Relax, you know your stuff. You are the expert. |
|  | Avoid jargon <br><br> • Don't use abbreviations or technical jargons. |

## Rules to Live by When Dealing with Reporters

Think before you speak. – Nothing is "off the record"

- Never LIE to a reporter

- Don't speculate or ramble especially in a crisis media interview

- Avoid saying "no comment." Find another way to deflect the question – especially in a crisis, the journalist will fill the gap

- Stay on the record

- Don't be offended by a reporter's ignorance;

- Don't be impatient with a reporter

- Don't accept definitions

- Never be argumentative, nasty or yell at a reporter. Keep calm.

- Avoid jargon. Think - how would I explain this to a friend not in my sector, without dumbing down or being patronising.

- Always be prepared for an interview

- Know what you are getting into

- Always have an agenda. Know what you want to achieve through this interview

## How to Carry Out Media Interviews

- Answer reporters' calls, or refer them to someone who will return their call if you are seeking media attention.

- Announce your own news first... even if it is bad news. Stay in control

- Don't demand to review a story before it is printed or aired

- If you have a statement, message or idea that must be understood, repeat it again, and again, and again.

# Some Frequently Asked Questions:

### Can I ask for the questions in advance?

Generally, the answer is no.

- However, more and more magazines, online media and print are now running Q&A interviews. In those instances, you will be sent the questions in advance for you to submit your response.

- I would say, whilst you may not be given the precise questions ahead of a broadcast interview, it is important you understand the area/theme for the interview, so ask beforehand.

### Can I have a copy of my contribution? (edited version or raw footage)

For most mainstream media outlets if you ask, they will generally send you a link to the version they have online. In the current climate to drive for more online interactivity, they will be happy for you to share item on your own social media platforms.

### Can I use it for social media?

With the importance of social media platforms, most would not object if you wanted to share your contribution on various platforms. It is highly likely the media outlet will be sharing on their own online platforms anyway e.g. their personal Twitter or Facebook accounts.

I hope you have found this helpful. Go ahead with confidence and achieve success handling those broadcast interviews.

Evadney Campbell

## Interviewing Tips Summary

Here are a few questions you should ask when you are approached to carry out an interview:

- Who is the reporter?
- How is the interview going to be used?
- Will you be part of a panel or just being interviewed by yourself?
- Are you being used for your expertise?
- Is this because of an incident/crisis?
- Will the interview be live or pre-recorded?

Once you have decided to do the interview, you need to be clear:

**What are your objectives?**

- What do you want to achieve from the interview?
- What are the key points you MUST hit in the interview?

**What is your message?** For broadcast I would advise, no more than about 3 key points.

- For TV you are likely to only have a few minutes if it is live.

- Keep your answers succinct 30 sec or shorter. Do not waffle, they will edit the interview and what may happen? You could lose your key message. Your answer may also be misinterpreted.

- Speak slowly – but not monotonous, vary your tone.

## How to Carry Out Media Interviews

- Relax, it is OK to use hand gestures if that is your normal way of speaking.

- Keep eye contact with the interviewer – it is a conversation.

- Keep it simple – refrain from using jargon.

For Radio length can be a little longer but again:

- It will depend on whether it is live or being recorded.

- If recorded, how will it be used – in full or as a clip.

- Smile when speaking – it will make you sound warm.

- Be passionate about your subject.

Practice, practice, practice. Get someone to do mock interviews with you. Fire questions at you from all corners. Make sure you do get your message across. Make sure you are the expert. Remember, use the 5 'Ws' and 'H' but throw in a few 'What ifs?"

See it as a 'Presentation' – You are only being interviewed but if you practice this you should not be side-lined by the interviewer.

Do not ad-lib, this is not the time to come up with something you have not pre-planned.

**REMEMBER**: - Nothing is "Off the record" with a reporter.

Always, make sure your personality comes through. Be yourself. This will make you appear much more engaging.

Have some relaxation techniques you can use before you go live.

Go over your talking point/messages a few times before you go live.

Release any tension in your body, shoulders - stretch, breathe!

## Training Opportunities:

- Shiloh PR offers a series of workshops to provide you with valuable tools and hands-on experience to inspire and build your knowledge in a practical way.

We will provide an excellent standard of training using course leaders with substantial media experience.

If you are interested in booking a place on any of our workshops listed below, or would perhaps like us to carry out a bespoke course for your network or employees, please get in touch using the **contact** form.

- Handling the Media during a Crisis
- Interviewing Techniques
- DIY PR Strategy
- Effective Customer Relations

# Creating an Effective PR Campaign: maximise your brand potential and media presence

- This training workshop will give delegates tips and practical exercises on how to develop your own public relations campaign including tips for creating an effective press release, using social media as well as ideas for gaining media attention for your business.

**Objectives: By the end of the course, you should be able to:**

- Identify the do's & don'ts of writing a press release• Compile a PR plan Write an email pitch Identify at least 5 different mediums to gain publicity. List at least 3 different social media sites.

**Session will include:**

- Writing a press release
- Using a template to create an email PR pitch
- Generating ideas for maximising opportunities for media coverage/exposure
- Tips to generate media attention
- Identifying key social media sites for promoting your business

## Who should attend?

- SMEs including sole traders who want to develop their own PR campaigns but cannot afford the services of a professional agency. It is also suitable for other executives who want a better understanding of how PR works.

Evadney Campbell

## Handling the Media During a Crisis

- This course aims to give you some tools to confidently handle the media during a crisis. This session will focus on interviews for broadcast, in live & pre-recorded situations, however, the principles will equally apply to print or online interviews.

- Given the growth and influence of social media, we will also identify some of the pitfalls of social media during a crisis and will give you a few suggestions of how to avoid or minimize these.

**Objectives:** By the end of the course, you should be able to:

- Create a basic crisis management plan for handling the media

- Conduct on the spot interview during a crisis

- Ensure your message is delivered and not that of the journalist

- Identify the different requirements for print or broadcast

- Using social media to control your message

**Session will include:**

- A presentation on tips for carrying out live on the spot interviews

## How to Carry Out Media Interviews

- Tips on handling the media in the immediate aftermath of a crisis
- Listening/viewing interviews how not to do it
- Discussing what went wrong and why - Listen/view good interviews
- Discuss why this went well
- Different needs of newspapers, radio, or TV news
- Learn about some of the key areas for consideration ahead of an interview
- Learn the 3 Rs for handling a crisis

**Who should attend?**

- Managers or senior staff members likely to be requested to do media interviews, particularly during a crisis.

Evadney Campbell

# Interviewing Techniques

- This course aims to give you some tools to help you confidently handle the media during an interview whether print or broadcast, in live & pre-recorded situations.

**Objectives:** By the end of the course, you should be able to:

- Carry out a studio based interview for TV or radio
- Carry out a field interview for radio or TV
- Ensure your message is delivered and not that of the journalist
- Recognise at least 3 broadcast media terminology
- Identify the different requirements for print or broadcast

**Session will include:**

- **Handling broadcast media interviews**

    - A presentation on tips for carrying out live/pre-recorded interviews
    - Guide on what to expect in radio & TV studios

## How to Carry Out Media Interviews

- Do's & Don'ts during a live broadcast interview

- Listening/viewing interviews how not to do it

- Discussing what went wrong and why - Listen/view good interviews

- Discuss why this went well

- Different needs of newspapers, radio, or TV news

- Learn about some of the key areas for consideration ahead of an interview

- Learn the 3 Rs for handling a crisis

**Who should attend?**

- Anyone who does media interviews – print, online or broadcast on behalf of their organisation, or anyone who prepares spokespeople for media interviews.

## Effective Customer Relations

- This course aims to give you the confidence to handle challenging customers to achieve a win-win outcome.

**Objectives:** By the end of the course, you will have:

- At least 3 tools to use when dealing with challenging customers
- Given tips for defusing potential conflict
- Identify potential solutions for most challenging issues
- Have fun

**Session will include:**

- **Essentials for good Customer Service**
  - Importance of good customer service
  - Tips to achieve excellent customer services

- **Practical Exercises 1**
  - Role play with external secret customer
  - Discuss how it was handled
  - What went well/How it could have been improved

- Feedback from 'secret customer'
- In groups, list areas of concern with potential solutions
- Each pair/group present their list & solutions
- Whole group discuss list and agree solutions

**Who should attend?**

- Anyone who has direct contact with customers/potential customers in person or via the telephone.

Evadney Campbell

# Consultation Packages

## Basic

This is a half hour telephone conversation during which we discuss the following. You will then be sent a written breakdown of discussion:

Current Position

- Where are you now?

Financial Goals

What would you like to be earning?

- Within the next 3 months

- Within the next 6 months

- Within the next 9 or 12 months

Business Objectives for the next:

- The next 3 months

- The next 9 months

- The next 12 months

Basic PR Strategy.

## Gold

One hour Skype/Telephone consultation where we will develop a personalised written plan of action, which covers the following for you:

Current Position

- Where are you now?

Financial Goals:

What would you like to be earning long-term?

- Within the next 3 months

- Within the next 6 months

- Within the next 9 to 12 months

Business Objectives for the next:

- 3 months

- 9 months

- 12 months

• Suggested PR Actions to take to achieve the above

• Draft PR Strategy

• PDF Interviewing Guideline

## Platinum

2 hrs Face to Face Consultation. You will be supplied with the above action plan in addition to the following:

Current Position

- Where are you now?

Financial Goals:

What would you like to be earning long-term?

- Within the next 3 months
- Within the next 6 months
- Within the next 9 to 12 months

Business Objectives for the next:

- 3 months
- 9 months
- 12 months

PR Strategy:

- Suggested PR Actions to take to achieve the above
- Press Release Template
- Assistance with 1st press release for up to a month

Evadney Campbell

- Five Specific media contacts

PDF of Broadcast Interviewing Guidebook

## Professional Advice/Assistance

For one-to-one media preparation training or PR consultation, contact:

### Evadney Campbell MBE:

Email: evadney@shilohpr.com

Twitter: twitter.com/evadneyc

LinkedIn: Linkedin.com/Evadney Campbell

### Shiloh PR:

Website: www.shilohpr.com,

Email: contact@shilohpr.com

Twitter: twitter.com/shilohpr

Facebook: Facebook.com/shilohpr

LinkedIn: Linkedin.com/company/Shiloh-pr

**Other titles in the series - coming soon:**

*"Guide to Crisis Communications"*

*"Using Social Media Effectively"*

Printed in Great Britain
by Amazon